Functional and Non-Functional Requirements *Simply Put!*

Simple Requirements Decomposition / Drill-Down Techniques for Defining IT Application Behaviors and Qualities

Thomas Hathaway
Angela Hathaway

Ordering Information:

Quantity sales. Special discounts are available on quantity purchases by corporations, associations, and others. For details, contact the publisher at books@BusinessAnalysisExperts.com.

The content of this book is also available as an eCourse at http://businessanalysisexperts.com/product/video-course-exposing-functional-and-non-functional-requirements/

ISBN-10: 1534983481
ISBN-13: 978-1534983489

DEDICATION

This work is dedicated to future generations of Business Analysts, Product Owners, Subject Matter Experts, Domain Experts, COOs, CEOs, Line Managers, and anyone responsible for representing the business community's interests on an Information Technology project.

CONTENTS

ACKNOWLEDGMENTS

This publication would not have been possible without the active support and hard work of our daughter, Penelope Hathaway. We would also be remiss if we did not acknowledge the thousands of students with whom we have had the honor of working over the years. We can honestly say that every single one of you influenced us in no small way.

Finally, we would like to acknowledge Harvey, the fictional Pooka created by Mary Chase and made famous by the movie of the same name with James Stewart. Very early in our marriage we recognized that a third entity is created and lives whenever we work closely on a concept, a new idea, or a new product. Over the years, this entity became so powerful and important to us that we decided to name it Harvey and he should rightfully be listed as the author of this and all of our creative works. Unfortunately, Harvey remains an invisible being, living somewhere beyond our physical senses but real nonetheless. Without Harvey, neither this book nor any of our other publications would have been possible. For us, Harvey embodies the entity that any collaborative effort creates and he is at least as real as each of us. We would truly be lost without him.

PREFACE

Defining solution-level requirements (aka functional and non-functional requirements) is a core competency for anyone in an organization responsible for defining future Information Technology (IT) applications. "Functional and Non-Functional Requirements – *Simply Put!*" will give

- ✓ Business Analysts,
- ✓ Systems Analysts,
- ✓ Agile Product Owners,
- ✓ Product Managers,
- ✓ Subject Matter Experts (a.k.a. SMEs),
- ✓ and really "anyone wearing the BA hat"

simple, repeatable techniques for extracting solution-level specifications from business and stakeholder requirements that are expressed in complete sentence form.

My co-author, Angela, and I have used these techniques on hundreds of IT projects around the globe and we know the value each provides. Using these approaches will improve your ability to identify and document requirements at the level of detail that solution providers (vendors or developers) need to deliver the right technology for their organization.

The presented techniques will work on any set of well-expressed requirement statements. However, they were specifically designed for and work best with requirement statements that follow the "Rules for Writing Effective Requirements" that we present in our course "Writing Requirements for IT – *Simply Put!*".

Regardless of your job title or role, if you are involved in defining future business solutions, this book will help you communicate your business needs to solution providers. It will reduce the potential for misunderstandings that undermine IT's ability to deliver the right technology for the business.

SKILLS:

Upon successful completion of this course, you can:

- ⇨ Decompose Business and Stakeholder Requirement Statements to identify Functional and Non-Functional Requirements
- ⇨ Give those responsible for designing, building, and/or buying the solution the kind of information they need to make the decisions that are right for the business
- ⇨ Identify Informational, Performance, and Constraining Requirements from a list of Functional Requirements
- ⇨ Document and manage Business, Stakeholder, Functional and Non-Functional Requirements
- ⇨ Capture and clarify Business Rules and External Constraints that mandate limits to the delivered solution
- ⇨ Develop measurable Solution Requirements that facilitate End-User Acceptance Testing

The course includes optional, online exercises with immediate feedback featuring our recommended resolution and the rationale behind it. At the end of the course, a "Final Exam' will allow you to test your understanding of how all of the presented ideas work together to make your requirements more easily understood by all respective target audiences.

Enjoy the learning experience! You can learn more business analysis techniques by visiting the Business Analysis Learning Store (http://businessanalysisexperts.com/business-analysis-training-store/) to see a wide selection of business analysis books, eCourses, virtual and face-to-face instructor-led training, as well as a selection of FREE Business Analysis training.

Meanwhile, please enjoy this book. We appreciate any comments, suggestions, recommended improvements, or complaints that you care to share with us. You can reach us via email at eBooks@businessanalysisexperts.com.

SETTING THE STAGE FOR REQUIREMENTS DECOMPOSITION

In today's wired world, business solutions almost always involve Information Technology (IT) components which someone will ultimately build, buy, modify, or adapt (most likely some combination thereof). IT applications are inherently complex and constant advances in technology increase that complexity.

The process of designing, developing, buying, and configuring an IT application involves a myriad of trade-off decisions. Developers, buyers, designers, and anyone involved in that process (collectively "**Solution Providers**") need to know what will satisfy all stakeholders to make the right decisions.

To deliver a solution that meets defined Business and Stakeholder Requirements, Solution Providers need a level of detail that they can easily understand and use to make appropriate design decisions.

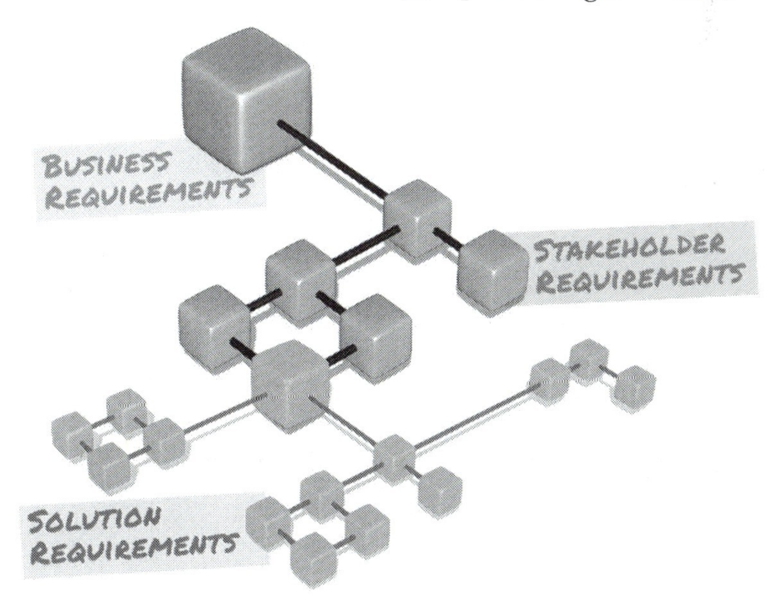

"Solution Requirements" provide that level of detail. (Our free, online video "What Are Requirements?" (http://businessanalysisexperts.com/product/what-are-business-requirements-stakeholder-solution/) provides an in-depth description of what Business, Stakeholder, and Solution Requirements are and how they define a proposed solution in increasing levels of detail.)

Simply stated, a Solution Requirement defines a ***function*** the solution will perform, ***data*** it will manipulate, a ***quality*** it will possess, OR a ***constraint*** it must meet.

By convention, there are two fundamentally different but related types of Solution Requirements for IT projects. "Functional Requirements" (FR) define functions with their related data while "Non-Functional Requirements" (NFR) define what Stakeholders consider acceptable qualities of the solution.

As the one wearing the BA hat, you need to understand how each of these four "dimensions" affects the delivered application. An effective Solution Requirement defines only one. You need to package the Solution Requirements into related sets that define all dimensions the Solution Providers need to deliver the right product.

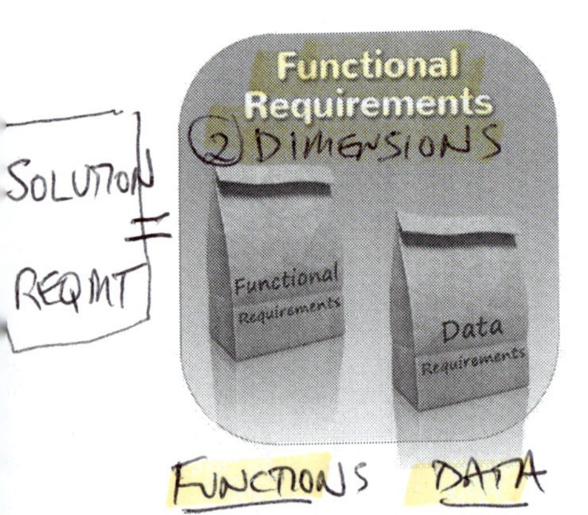

Here is an example to clarify exactly what this means using a Stakeholder Requirement that meets all of our previously defined rules (i.e., it is a simple, complete, well-structured sentence that states the business outcome, targets components that are in scope, and is clear to the target audience):

STAKEHOLDER REQUIREMENT

SHR23: "To make responsible financial decisions, the Chief Financial Officer (CFO) needs to know the Projected Net Income (PNI) for the upcoming 12-month period."

Although this statement is sufficient from the business perspective, it might not be clear to the Solution Providers. Any application that satisfies this *Stakeholder Requirement* also has to satisfy *Solution Requirements*. Following is an excerpt of the Solution Requirements that are contained in the above Stakeholder Requirement:

SOLUTION REQUIREMENTS

F231: Calculate Projected Net Income (Function)
D987: Projected Gross Income (Data)
D994: Projected Expenditures (Data)
D011: Current Date (Data)
U895: Cash Forecast Window (User View)
...
BR687: rolling 12-month period
(NFR - this will become a business rule; more on that later)
S681: Limit access to CFO (NFR - Security requirement)
...

This set is obviously incomplete as you could extract many other

Functional and Non-Functional Requirements from this Stakeholder Requirement. It serves here only to illustrate the level of detail that Solution Providers need to do their job.

As noted earlier, Solution Providers face an immense number of decisions on how a future business solution will work and each decision has consequences that are difficult to foresee. For example, there are many different ways to implement the "Calculate Projected Net Income" function and each way has its own pros and cons. The selected way will impact the workflow of several people significantly (e.g., Sales, Finance, and Budgeting departments). There is no question as to whether these decisions will be made. The only questions are WHO makes the decisions and WHEN do they make them.

Organizational factors such as job titles, roles, and responsibilities, skills of the individuals on a project, and the type of Software Development Methodology (SDM) will determine WHO should discover this level of detail and WHEN they should do it.

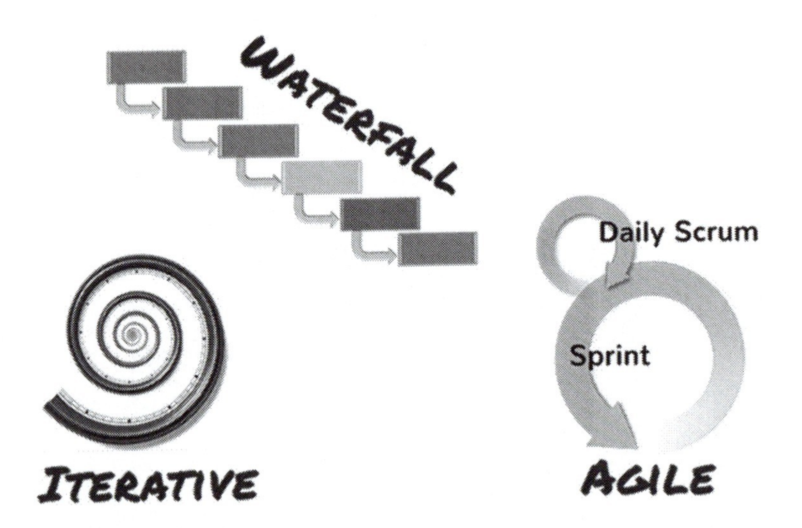

The default is always the individual who needs the decision to finish his or her job, namely the Solution Provider. The question now becomes whether that individual should be making decisions that have a significant impact on the success of the project and the future of the business. We recommend assigning this responsibility to someone who represents the business community. Solution requirements give the

Solution Providers the guidance they need to make their technical decisions *in the best interest of the business community*.

WHEN to define Solution Requirements depends on the SDM you use. In a “Waterfall”, “Iterative”, or “Structured” approach, the one wearing the BA hat does it before finalizing the requirements.

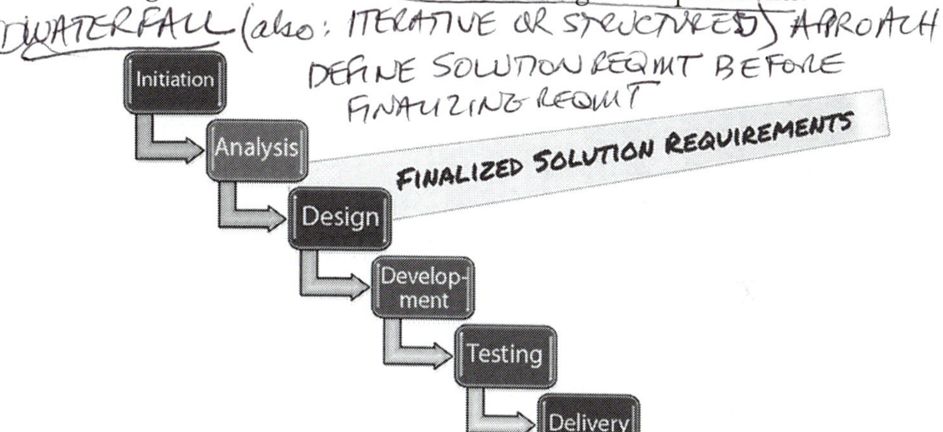

In an Agile setting, developers will usually identify Solution Requirements for the IT component when they start to code a specific user story/work item.

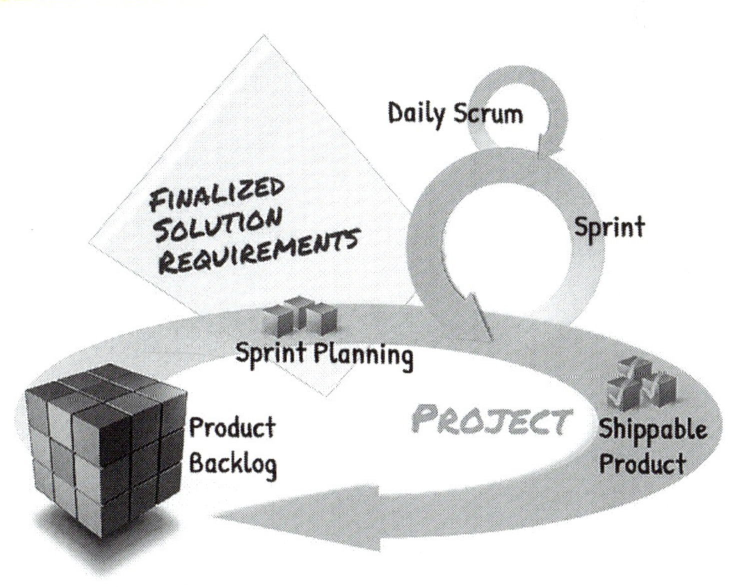

Regardless who defines Solution Requirements and when they do it, Solution Providers need a sense of direction in all four dimensions (***functions, data, qualities, and constraints***) for each requirement to guide their decision-making process. The critical question is HOW to get from Business and Stakeholder Requirement statements to the Solution Requirement level.

We will introduce you to a technique for extracting explicit and implied Solution Requirements (both Functional and Non-Functional) from a requirement statement. The technique starts with the functional dimension and progresses toward the Non-Functional dimensions (data, qualities, and constraints) later. This ensures that the technique is repeatable and verifiable to minimize missing Solution. Requirements.

Online resources for you:

- FREE video: What Are Requirements?
  http://businessanalysisexperts.com/product/what-are-business-requirements-stakeholder-solution/

- Scaled Agile Framework: Nonfunctional Requirements
  http://scaledagileframework.com/nonfunctional-requirements/

- IIBA BABOK Requirements Classification Scheme
  http://www.iiba.org/babok-guide/babok-guide-v2/babok-guide-online/chapter-one-introduction/1-3-key-concepts.aspx

- Explain how BABOK categorizes requirements
  http://www.modernanalyst.com/Careers/InterviewQuestions/tabid/128/ID/2033/Explain-how-BABOK-categorizes-requirements.aspx

- What Requirements Documents Does A Business Analyst Create?
  http://www.bridging-the-gap.com/what-requirements-specifications-do-business-analysts-create/

DISCOVERING FUNCTIONAL AND INFORMATIONAL REQUIREMENTS

This chapter will help you:

- Understand the Purpose of Functional Requirements
- Identify and Define Functional Requirements
- Document Functional Requirements
- Understand the Purpose of Informational Requirements
- Explain the Relationship between Functional and Informational Requirements
- Identify and Define Informational Requirements
- Document Informational Components
- Understand Usability Requirements and User Views
- Identify and Define Data Elements
- Define Algorithms for Derivable Data
- Specify Data Element Accuracy

Capturing Functional Requirements

Functions are the heart and soul of every IT solution. Unless the software ***does*** something, it has no value. You can name any Functional Requirement using the "verb object" form. More specifically,

⇨ **use an active verb** (one that states the action)

⇨ **and direct objects** (the things the action creates or affects)

(e.g., "Calculate Sales Tax", "Verify Order", and "Identify Caller"). By naming the function this way, the name expresses what the function actually does.

A Business or Stakeholder Requirement often blatantly states or implies functions.

Business Requirement

"We will reduce order entry errors by 80% by December 31, 2015"

is a valid Business Requirement. It states one function "Reduce Order Entry Errors" but implies many others (e.g., "Count Order Entry Errors", "Calculate Error Rate", "Compare Current Error Rate to Baseline Rate"). The requirement,

Stakeholder Requirement

"To reduce order entry errors, customers can only select items that are in stock"

That Stakeholder Requirement states the function "Select Item" and implies the functions "Check Item Inventory", "Reserve Ordered Item", etc. Too often, these "hidden" functions are neglected because the author "assumes" they will be delivered. Beware! In those woods be dragons!

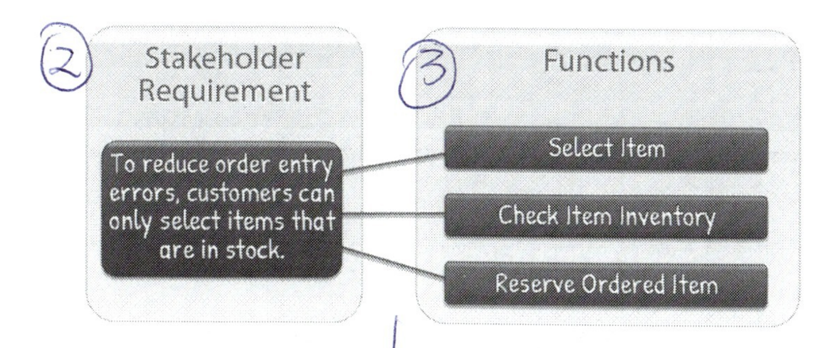

As the one wearing the BA hat, your job includes defining all ***automated and manual*** functions that the proposed solution will have to perform to satisfy ***all*** Business and Stakeholder Requirements.

Start identifying functions by listing those that are obvious. For example,

> "The application should calculate the premium discount for safe drivers."

This requirement blatantly expresses the function "Calculate Premium Discount", so it is a good starting point. Next, look for not-so-obvious or implied functions. By definition, a discount is a percentage taken off a base amount. That implies that the application has to know the premium to be able to "Calculate a Premium Discount".

Furthermore, the requirement refers to "safe drivers" as a group of people who apparently qualify for this premium discount. How can the application recognize a "safe driver"? In discussing this with the SME, I discover that a safe driver is one who has not had an accident or traffic violation in 3 years. Based on this information, I realize that I need a function to evaluate the driving record of the applicant to determine whether they fit this profile, ergo the function, "Evaluate Driving Record".

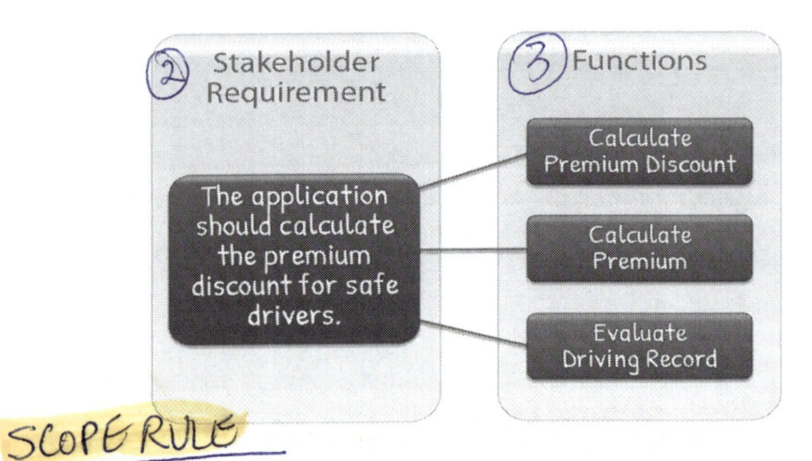

As soon as I get into these not-so-obvious functions, I have to make sure that I am staying within the scope of my project and not violating the scope rule.

For instance, based on the SME's answer to my previous question, I might conclude that the application has to "Track Accident History" and "Track Traffic Violations", which would be two great hitherto hidden functions. Fortunately, the SME informs me that individual state governments have a "Department of Motor Vehicles (DMV)" that performs these functions and the driving record is available via a web service from each state agency. Thankfully, the tracking functions are out of scope for my project.

The process we are describing is "requirement decomposition" or "requirement drill-down". It will ultimately generate **functional, informational, quality, and constraining requirements** that you can package to provide the appropriate level of detail for Solution Providers. Because nothing is as simple as it appears at first glance, trying it out could reveal some hidden complexity. That implies that it is time for an exercise.

Exercise: Decomposing Requirements to Functions

All exercises in this book are optional. They are online exercises that take anywhere from a few minutes to 20 minutes.

This particular exercise will give you an opportunity to test your ability to find functions based on complete sentence requirements. For each presented requirement, simply type the functions you can identify into the text area provided. Separate each function with a comma and a space and click on the "Submit" button when you are ready to compare your answers with what we think.

To start the exercise, please go to http://goo.gl/LdTKOl

*(**DISCLAIMER**: If you attempt the exercises on a standard PC, please use IE10 or higher or Chrome. They may not work on FireFox.)*

Documenting Functions

Now that you know how to find functional elements in a requirement statement, what do you do with them? The obvious answer is "document them." It is great for your understanding of the requirement that you know what functions are stated or implied, but this is the very kind of information that Solution Providers need to be able to deliver the right solution. Some of them might think of many of these things anyway, but may not think of all of them.

You captured the functions in a list connected to the requirement statement from which you derived them. Beyond the Verb-Object name, you should also have a unique identifier for each function such as a running number prefixed with the letter "F" to indicate that it is a functional component (there will be other types of components added later). For example:

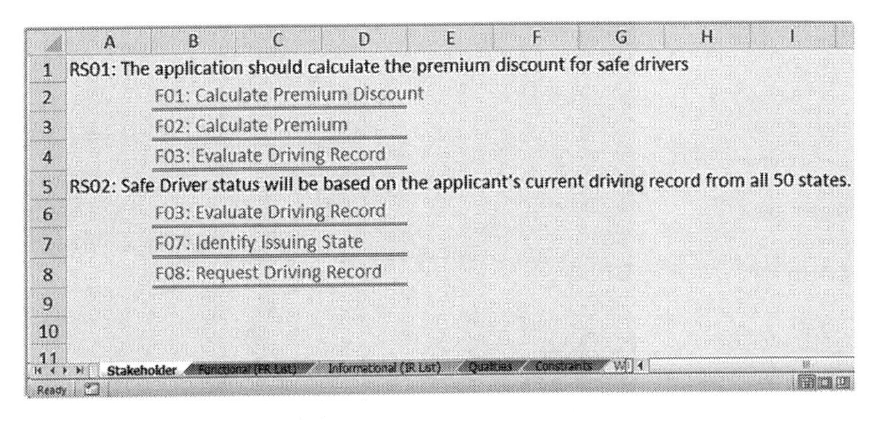

	A	B	C	D	E	F	G	H	I
1	RS01: The application should calculate the premium discount for safe drivers								
2		F01: Calculate Premium Discount							
3		F02: Calculate Premium							
4		F03: Evaluate Driving Record							
5	RS02: Safe Driver status will be based on the applicant's current driving record from all 50 states.								
6		F03: Evaluate Driving Record							
7		F07: Identify Issuing State							
8		F08: Request Driving Record							
9									
10									
11									

Stakeholder | Functional (FR List) | Informational (IR List) | Qualities | Constraints

As you can see in this example, the unique identifier (e.g., F03) is independent of the requirement statement (RS01 and RS02) from which it came. If you discover the same function in multiple requirement statements, give it the same name and number in each. To facilitate this, you need a separate, searchable "Functional Requirements List" ("FR List") – in which all identified functions from all requirement statements appear only.

By sorting the FR List alphabetically by name, it is relatively easy to figure out whether or not you have already listed a specific function and to get the unique identifier for it. If you do not create a separate

FR List, you will have to repeat the same data, qualities, and constraints (more on that later) everywhere the function is listed. That creates redundancy leading to inconsistencies over time.

Capturing Informational Requirements

All functions use, create, modify, delete, or present data. Requirements at all levels of detail often refer to data but "assume" that the Solution Providers are responsible for figuring out what data the requirement needs and what data it creates. After all, before they were called "Information Technology" they were (and in some organizations still are) called "Data Processing". The fallacy persists that data is the IT group's or Data Administration's concern and not important to the business community. Nothing could be further from the truth.

Actually, the term "data" can be misleading. You need to concern yourself with all "Informational Components" to develop a complete set of requirements for a proposed business solution. Informational Components can be either "User Views" (e.g. reports, screens, windows, web pages, audio files, video files, text files, databases) or individual "Data Elements".

A User View is simply a collection of Data Elements. A Data Element is "atomic data", meaning data in its simplest form. For example, a User View of "Customer Address" in the United States typically consists of a Customer Name, Street Address, City, State, and Zip Code. The latter are Data Elements whereas the "Customer Address" is a User View that allows anyone to locate the customer geographically. The Customer Address provides the value that the user needs.

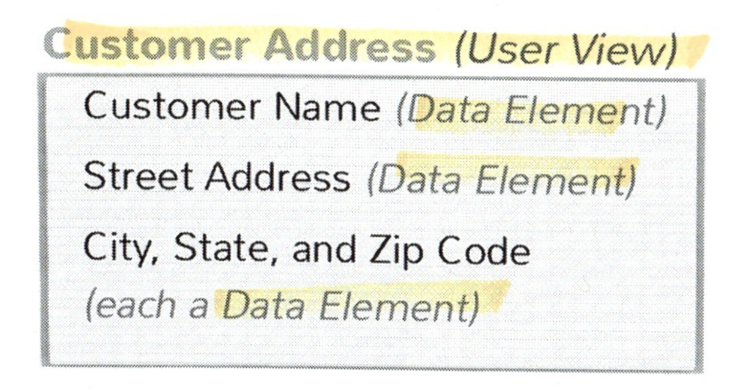

As the one wearing the BA hat, you are responsible for identifying and defining every Informational Component of the proposed business solution. You can find them by considering what information each function needs and what information it provides.

To identify User Views and Data Elements, you need to ask two simple questions for each function:

⇨ What data does the function produce when it is performed?

⇨ What data does the function need to provide that outcome?

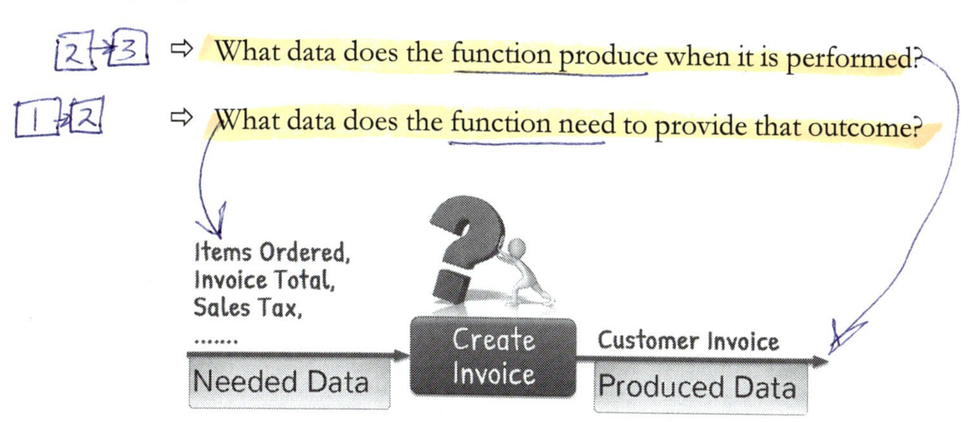

Start with the Functional Requirements List that you created and identify related Data Elements and User Views for each function. You might want to create a list showing all requirement statements mentioning that specific function to make sure you identify as many Informational Components as possible.

The function "Calculate Premium" could require a thundering herd of Data Elements and User Views, but assume that it will need the applicant's date of birth (DOB) — since automotive insurance is usually considerably higher for younger drivers. If the policy includes coverage for the insured party's own vehicle (i.e. collision of comprehensive coverage), the function "Calculate Premium" will also probably need vehicle data, like the age of the vehicle, current value of the vehicle, replacement value of the vehicle, etc.

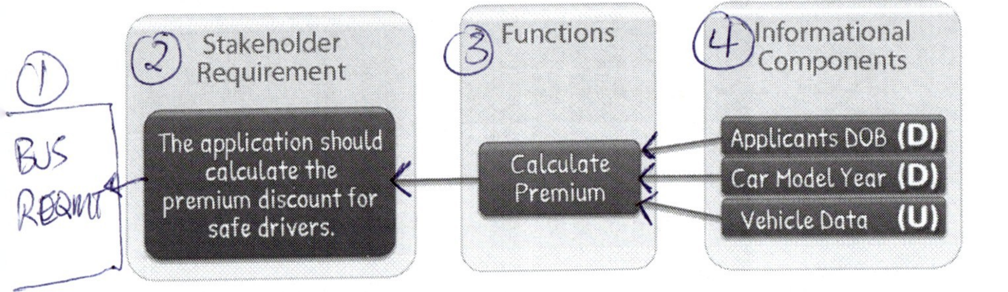

These Data Elements might not be as obvious as the previous example, so they may require both some analytic legwork and domain knowledge. Data is one of the biggest problems for a project and one that is very expensive to fix later if it is wrong. A good practice is to make sure that you have identified as many of the Data Elements that will be part of your solution as you possibly can.

Finally, for the "Evaluate Driving Record" function, we already know from the SME that laws require respective state agencies to maintain that type of information, so what you need to know for this function is how to get the information from them. What data do you have to provide the state agencies to get a driving record?

You presumably need the driver's license number and the issuing state. You could call what the respective DMV returns an "Incident Log" because it is a User View that lists any traffic violations, citations, or accidents reported for the driver. Each incident on it is also a User View because it is a collection of Data Elements about the incident. The driver's license number is a Data Element used to identify a specific driver.

Exercise: Discovering Informational Components

All exercises in this book are optional. They are online exercises that take anywhere from a few minutes to 20 minutes.

This exercise will give you an opportunity to test your ability to find Informational Components based on a list of functions. For each presented function, simply type the related Informational Components you can identify into the text area. Separate each entry with a comma and a space for best results. Click on the "Submit" button when you are ready for us to compare your answers with what we think.

To start the exercise, please go to http://goo.gl/iCPMIh

(***DISCLAIMER:*** *If you attempt the exercises on a standard PC, please use IE10 or higher or Chrome. They may not work on FireFox.)*

Attributes of Informational Requirements

Documenting Informational Components

In "Documenting Functions", you initiated the Functional Requirements List (FR List) with unique identifiers for each function. Now, add the relevant Informational Components (User Views and Data Elements) that you identified beneath the related function.

This is the first step in the expansion of the FR List in which we add the Data Dimension. Each Informational Component needs a unique identifier that is ***independent*** of the function and an indicator distinguishing User Views (U) from Data Elements (D). You will need it later.

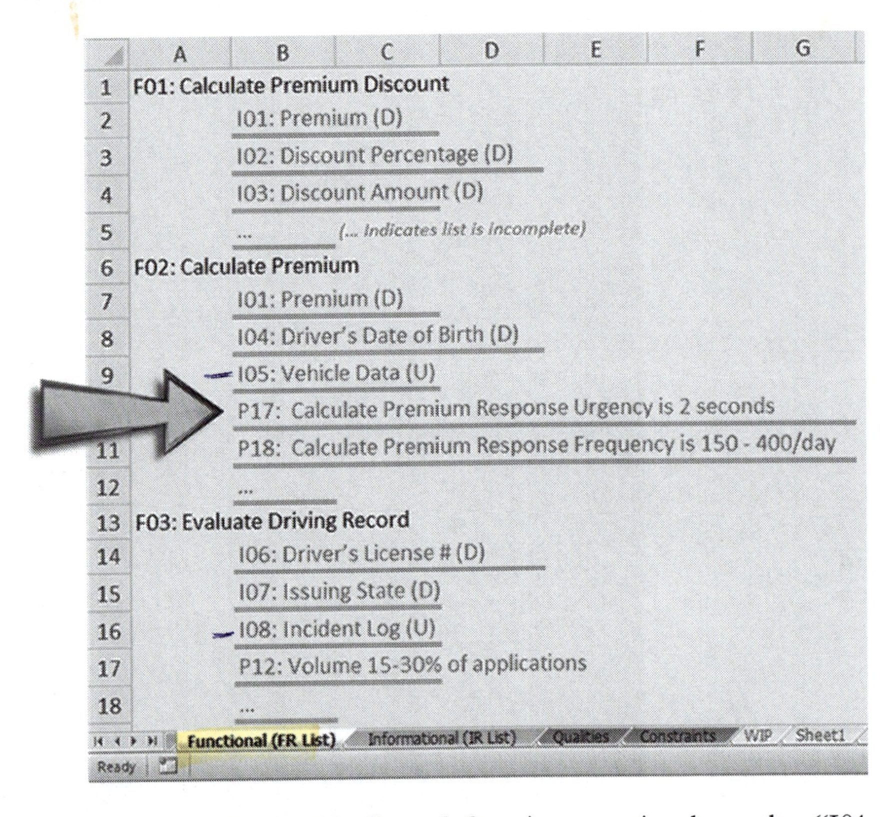

	A	B	C	D	E	F	G
1	**F01: Calculate Premium Discount**						
2		I01: Premium (D)					
3		I02: Discount Percentage (D)					
4		I03: Discount Amount (D)					
5		...	(... Indicates list is incomplete)				
6	**F02: Calculate Premium**						
7		I01: Premium (D)					
8		I04: Driver's Date of Birth (D)					
9		I05: Vehicle Data (U)					
		P17: Calculate Premium Response Urgency is 2 seconds					
11		P18: Calculate Premium Response Frequency is 150 - 400/day					
12		...					
13	**F03: Evaluate Driving Record**						
14		I06: Driver's License # (D)					
15		I07: Issuing State (D)					
16		I08: Incident Log (U)					
17		P12: Volume 15-30% of applications					
18		...					

Functional (FR List) | Informational (IR List) | Qualities | Constraints | WIP | Sheet1

Ready

As you go down this list of functions, notice how the "I01 Premium" is listed under functions "F01: Calculate Premium Discount" and "F02: Calculate Premium". In both instances, they have the same identifiers. Of course, on this short list, the duplicity is easy to see. Since the FR List can grow quickly, we strongly recommend maintaining a separate, searchable list of **all** Informational Components.

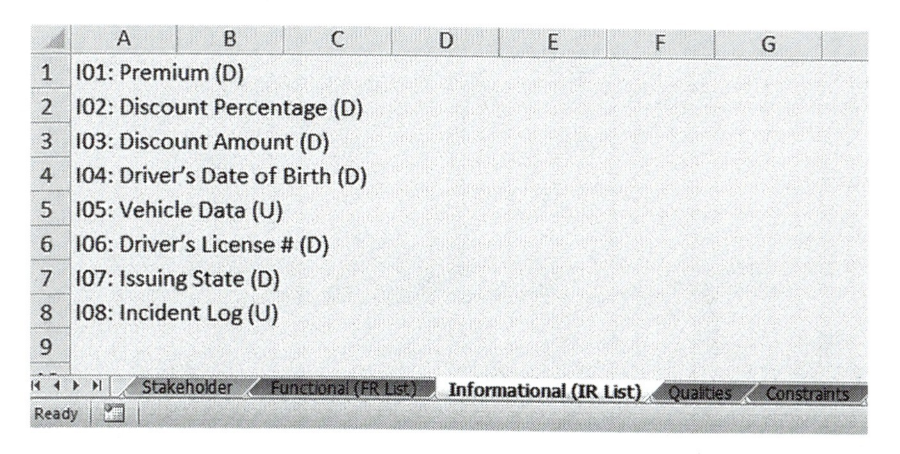

We call this the "Informational Requirements List" – or simply the "IR List". Like the FR List, you will expand the IR List by adding qualities of and constraints for the Informational Components.

Usability Requirements Define User Views

User Views are where people meet technology. Given the capabilities of modern applications, User Views are not just "interfaces" where data is displayed but can include sophisticated "interactions" (e.g., moving objects on the screen, navigating menus).

Solution Providers need to know the expectations of the people who will be using the application. To ensure that the users will be satisfied with the delivered solution, the one wearing the BA hat needs to define Usability Requirements for each User View.

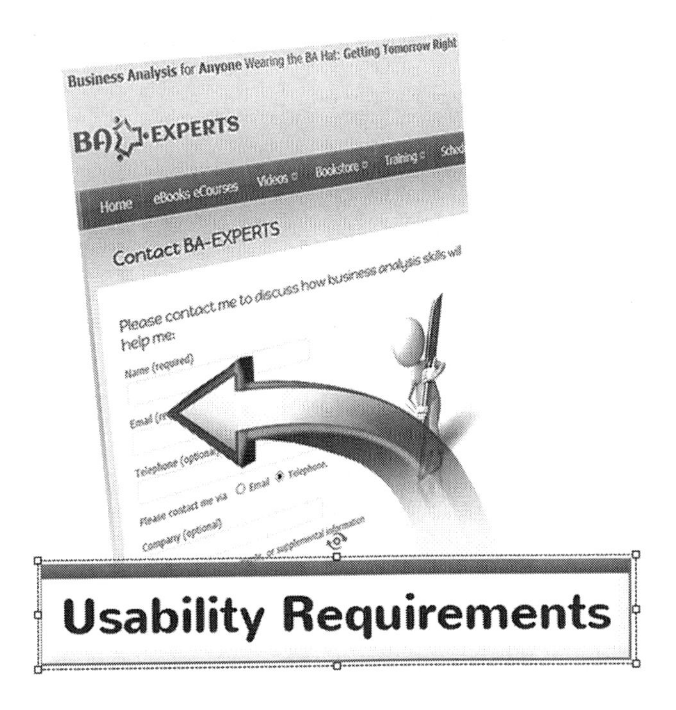

Usability is a critical, non-functional dimension for any application that involves human interaction (e.g., web apps, data entry applications, and dashboards). Solution providers need usability requirements defining the target audiences including aspects such as their:

- ☑ level of comfort with the technology (high, medium, low)
- ☑ desired experience with the application (quick in-and-out, rich content, mixed)
- ☑ how often they will be using it (occasionally, regularly, constantly)
- ☑ knowledge about the subject matter the application supports (Novice, Experienced, Expert)

To define Usability Requirements, extract User Views from your Informational Requirements List.

Here is an example of the User View "Incident Log" with its relevant Usability Requirements:

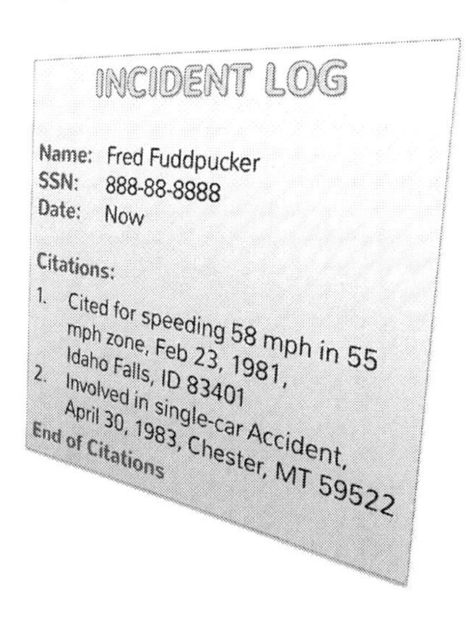

Usability Requirements for Incident Log User View:

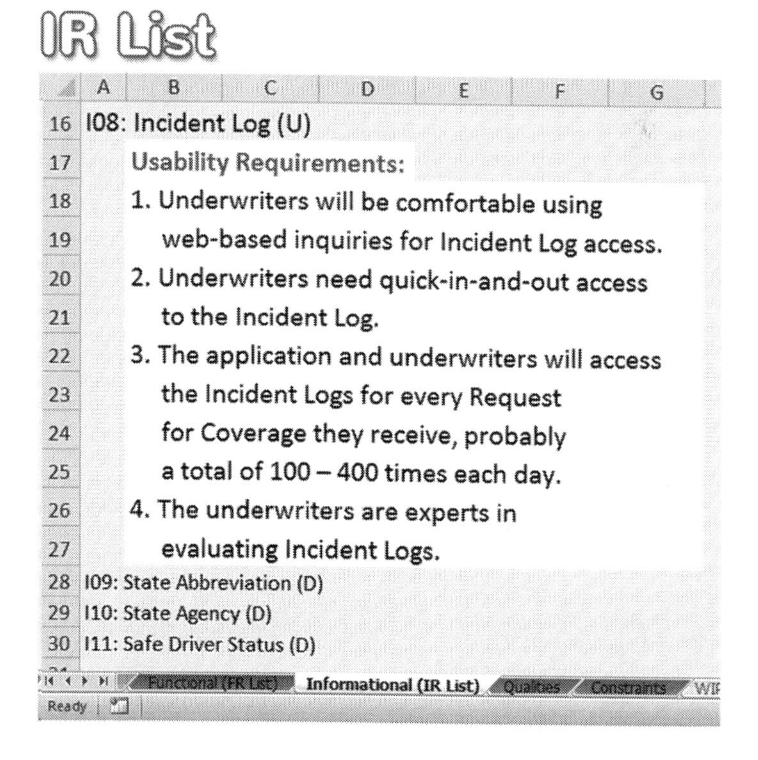

Beyond Usability Requirements, User Views might also need references to potential guidelines, templates, or standard layouts restricting the design options. You may have to identify internal and external constraints that affect the User View (more on this later).

Defining Data Elements

You identified individual Data Elements while you were "Finding Informational Components", earlier. In addition, every User View contains Data Elements that the business community needs. Since missing *business data* is one of the costliest errors for applications, you should do your best to identify and define ALL relevant aspects of ALL business Data Elements before giving your requirements list to the Solution Developers.

As a result, you can discover a humungous number of Data Elements and defining each of them could start to look like a Herculean task.

The good news is that this may not be your responsibility. Many modern organizations have a "Data Administration" group responsible for Corporate Data. Other organizations have "Data Analysts" whose sole responsibility is to maintain consistent definitions of all Data Elements the business community needs. Check with the respective data groups before you spend any time adding attributes to the Data Elements on your Informational Requirements List.

The number and variety of attributes that define each Data Element are too numerous for inclusion here. However, we want to mention two critical attributes that Solution Providers need the business community to define (either specifically for your project or from the respective data group), namely Algorithms for Data Elements the application will produce and their respective Accuracy.

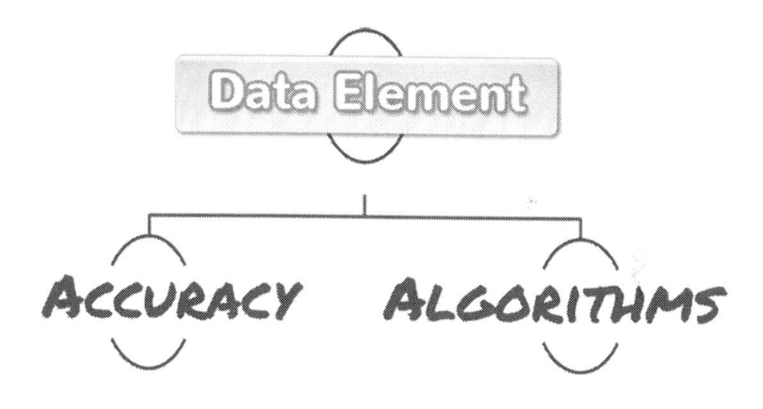

Algorithms for Derivable Data

You need to let the Solution Providers know the business algorithm for any Data Element your application calculates (in technical terms "Derivable Data").

For example, APPLICANT_AGE is derivable given the Applicant's date of birth and today's date. That formula is simple, but unless you specify it in the definition of the Data Element APPLICANT_AGE, the Solution Providers might have their own interpretation. (*Interestingly, some organizations are legally required to calculate age by rounding it up if you are less than 6 months from your next birthday. That begs the question, 'How old are you really?*) Here is a somewhat more complex example:

Add the Algorithm for any derivable Data Element to your Informational Requirements List to ensure that the Solution Providers get it right.

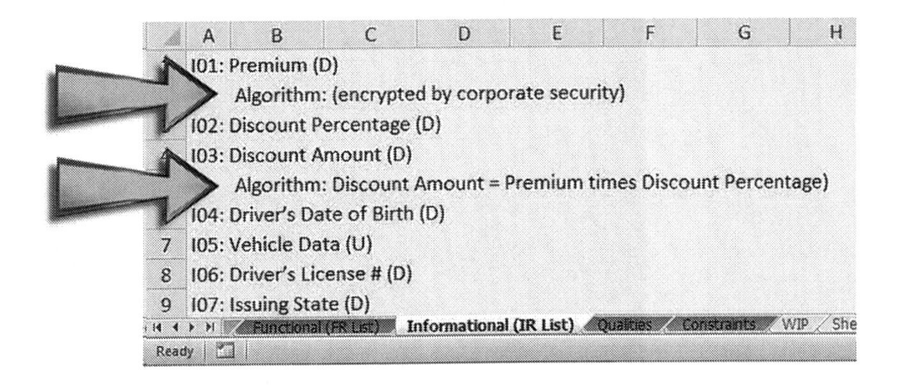

As a side note, you should also work with the aforementioned data groups to get their acceptance of your requirement.

Data Element Accuracy

The business community has to define the acceptable *accuracy* of their business data — and nothing is 100% accurate. To be considered accurate, each Data Element has to contain the most up-to-date (**current**) value at the required level of **precision** that satisfies the business need.

In the world of requirements, the term "**currency**" is a measure of time. It measures how quickly information changes in the real world have to be available to the application from the business perspective. For the On-Hand Quantity to be current in an inventory control application, you might need to reduce the value as soon as a sale is final and increase it as soon as the Receiving department has processed a shipment containing that item. In an accounting application, it is typically sufficient if the accounts are updated monthly whereas in a cash-forecasting model, it might be current enough if the data reflects income from the last quarter.

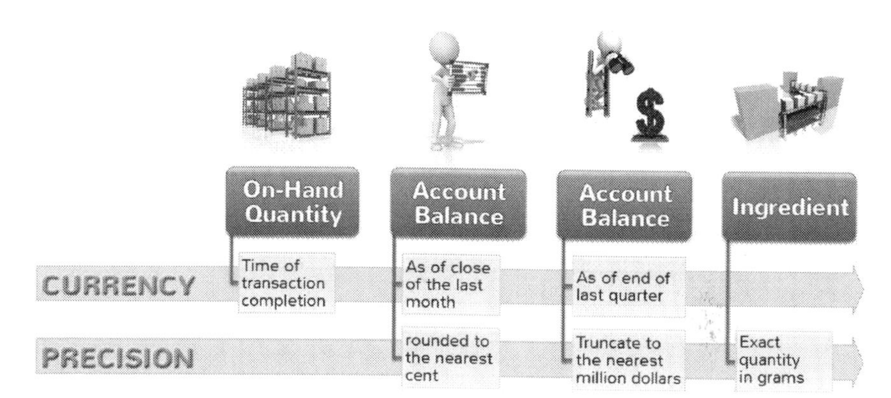

Accounting applications are typically **precise** to the nearest cent (i.e. two places beyond the decimal point). Manufacturing applications may require data precise to the nearest gram, or pound, or ton, obviously dependent upon what they manufacture and in what quantities. Cash forecasting applications may require precision to the nearest million dollars. Determining the level of precision for each Data Element is a business decision. Knowing when to round calculated results and when to truncate them are both key to attaining the required level of precision

If you already have precision and currency defined from a previous function that used this Data Element, confirm with your SME that the answers have not changed. This way, if different functions require different degrees of accuracy or currency, you will be able to quickly identify this and get a resolution from the subject matter experts.

Exercise: Assessing Precision and Currency

All exercises in this book are optional. They are online exercises that take anywhere from a few minutes to 20 minutes.

In this exercise, you can test your understanding of accuracy requirements based on two common financial applications, accounting and cash forecasting. You do not need any knowledge of either type of application for this exercise. Simply read the provided background information and use it to select the most appropriate responses to the questions.

To start the exercise, please go to http://goo.gl/AQvHsB

(***DISCLAIMER***: *If you attempt the exercises on a standard PC, please use IE10 or higher or Chrome. They may not work on FireFox.)*

Summary of Functional Requirements

In summary, Solution Providers need to know the anticipated Volumes, Precision, Accuracy, Formula (for Derivable Data), and Source (for Base Data) of every new data element the business community to see. If you as the one wearing the BA hat do not deliver this information, you are leaving it up to the Solution Providers to determine what the business will get.

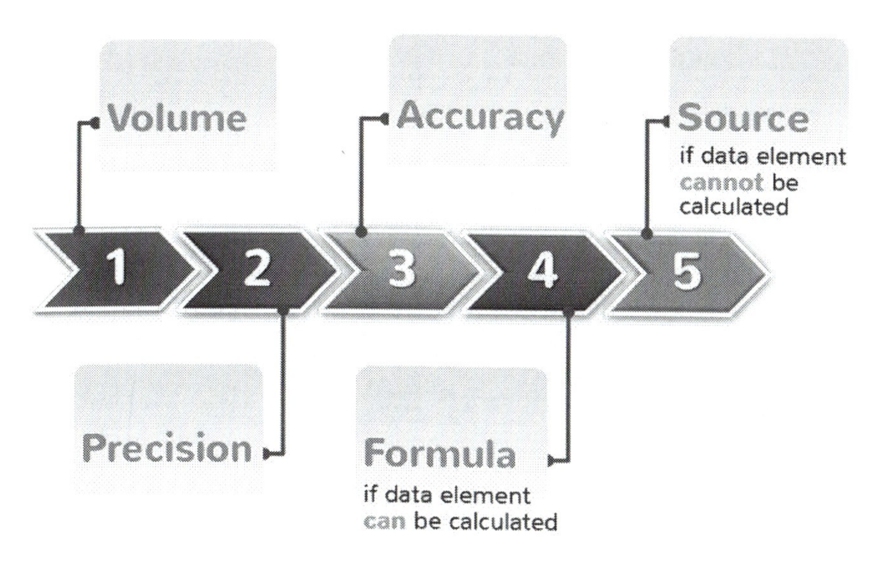

Online resources for you:

- ⇨ FREE Business Analysis Videos
  http://businessanalysisexperts.com/product-category/free-business-analysis-training/

- ⇨ What Goes into a Functional Specification?
  http://www.bridging-the-gap.com/functional-specification/

- ⇨ Decomposition – Functional and Otherwise
  http://www.bawiki.com/wiki/techniques/decomposition-functional-and-otherwise/

- ⇨ An Agile Functional Specification
  http://www.its-all-design.com/an-agile-functional-specification/

- ⇨ What's really going on when you decompose a requirement?
  https://www.ibm.com/developerworks/community/blogs/requirementsmanagement/resource/clip_image0067.jpeg?lang=en

- ⇨ An Agile Functional Specification
  http://www.its-all-design.com/an-agile-functional-specification/

- ⇨ What Is a Use Case
  https://www.youtube.com/watch?v=nN7ITDWKP6g

- ⇨ What Exactly Is Requirements Elicitation
  https://www.youtube.com/watch?v=vSXn16qMEZo

- ⇨ Business Data Modeling: Getting Informational Requirements for IT
  https://www.youtube.com/watch?v=0ZAP2y5PFNc

CAPTURING NON-FUNCTIONAL SOLUTION REQUIREMENTS

This chapter will help you:

- Understand the Need for Performance Requirements
- Explain Common Types of Performance Requirements
- Define Common Performance Measures
- Identify Internal and External Constraints

You now have identified a thundering herd (more or less) of things the software will do (Functions) and information it needs or creates (Data). Because functions need data and data can only be manipulated by functions, those two dimensions form inseparable pairs. As a result, (and for historical reasons), the category "Functional Requirements" commonly encompasses both.

So where do the ubiquitous "Non-Functional Requirements" come in? Since these define qualities that any solution must possess and they are related to some level of Functional Requirements, it is easiest to think about Non-Functional Requirements once you have identified a lot of the Functional Requirements. Once you have a good list of functions and data, you can ask a sequence of questions about each component to identify these pesky non-functional dimensions. This approach significantly reduces the potential for missing requirements.

Performance Requirements

Performance Requirements are a critical type of Non-Functional Requirements simply because failure to meet them is an all-too-common cause of project failures. Daily newspapers and TV news constantly report on IT applications that are unable to handle the volume of transactions they had to face.

One example is the https://healthcare.gov website. A total debacle when initially opened to the public, the website still has a long way to go before its performance satisfies demand. A not quite so recent example is a website upgrade by a well-known encyclopedia producer. The site was highly touted as offering the latest and greatest in features and functions, but when they went live, it took about 4 hours before all of their servers were overloaded or crashed. They were forced to uninstall the upgrade, go back to the old site, and redevelop the new site (which took months of development time). To say the least, it was not good publicity for the organization.

The question is not whether you need Performance Requirements, but rather who is responsible for them: the business community, the one wearing the BA hat, or the Solution Providers?

The correct answer is all three. Solution Providers are obviously involved in getting the technology to work fast enough to meet the highest expected traffic, but it is the business community's job to anticipate just how high that is. The one wearing the BA hat has to capture, clarify, and confirm the requirements and has to emphasize the importance of Performance Requirements to the business community. Assuming that performance will take care of itself has proven to be a high-risk endeavor for many projects in many organizations.

Effective Performance Requirements define acceptable behavior for the application *in measurable terms.* When you ask a SME, "How fast?" or "How many", they often respond with, "very fast" or "a lot". The problem with those answers is, of course, that it is impossible to measure them. (Just how many is "a lot", anyway?) You need to distinguish between *measurable* Performance Requirements and *subjective* Performance Requirements.

Measurable Performance Requirements are numbers (as in, "10,000 transactions per hour", or "one second response time", or as our example shows, simply "a 6-pack") that a third party can objectively measure and evaluate.

Subjective Performance Requirements, on the other hand, contain words like, "easy to", "high quality", or - if you are a beer drinker - "good beer" that require human assessment. That means that only the author of the requirement (if anyone) can determine whether the solution meets the requirement — and only once he or she has access to the solution.

These requirements are valid performance needs from the business perspective but to be usable as requirements, you need to quantify them. Quantifying a requirement means transforming a Subjective Performance Requirement into a Measurable Performance Requirement. To be able to deliver a solution that satisfies the Business and Stakeholder Requirements, Solution Providers need to know in measurable terms what satisfies the business community.

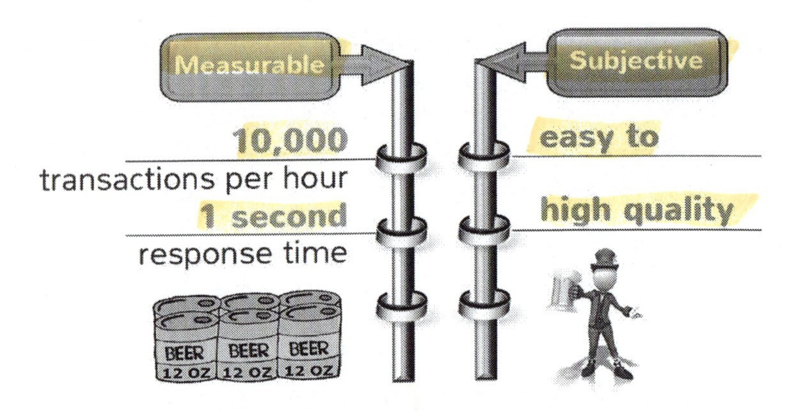

How can you recognize a subjective requirement and how can you translate it into measurable terms? The answer is not simple. The following table contains a few potential categories of subjective requirements and examples of expressing them in measurable terms:

USABILITY is a very common subjective requirement for just about any application with human interaction. The most overused requirements for these types of applications include the use of the term "user friendly". I have no idea what someone else considers user friendly. I know what I consider user friendly, but I am a geek. What I think of as "user friendly" others consider "user hostile". To translate the user-friendly quality into a measurable requirement, you need to specify an observable aspect that a third party could test.

For example, *"Experienced underwriters should require no more than a one-day introductory seminar to process Internet applications."*

TRAINABILITY (aka learnability) defines how quickly a new user needs to be able to utilize the application (i.e., "The policy maintenance application has to be easy to learn.") You need to find a measurable behavior that satisfies the trainability quality. A common measure of trainability is the length of time that it should take a qualified individual to reach a predetermined proficiency.

For example, *"Experienced underwriters should require no more than a one-day introductory seminar to process Internet applications."*

FLEXIBILITY has become very important in recent years based on the booming increase in business that some organizations experience because of effective marketing. This quality typically refers to a range in the volume of data, transactions, or users that the solution should be able to support without requiring redesign or Solution Provider intervention.

For example, *"The application will support a 10-fold increase in visitor traffic."*

AVAILABILITY is a measure of when the solution has to be available for users. It is a common requirement for on-line or web-based applications. Whereas uninterrupted, 24-hour availability might seem like a good idea, the expense of actually making that happen can be prohibitive.

For example, a realistic measure could be more like, *"Customer Service will be available for live chats 6am – 10pm EST Mon – Fri."."*

RELIABILITY of software is immensely important in mission-critical applications or in environments where peoples' lives depend on the technology (soldiers in a war zone, hospital patients, etc.). You need to ask two specific questions to define Reliability Requirements:

1. What is the minimum acceptable amount of time the

application has to run without interruption? The answer to this question is called the "Mean Time between Failures (MTBF)".

2. When the application is down, what is the maximum acceptable amount of time before it has to be restored? This answer represents the "Mean Time to Repair (MTTR)".

Minimum acceptable time?

Mean Time Between Failures

Maximum acceptable time?

Mean Time To Repair

For example, a simple Reliability Requirement is,
"The MTBF for the nuclear power plant radiation level monitor is one year and the MTTR is 1 shift."

The key point regarding subjective Performance Requirements is that these are business concerns and the business community has to define them before the project gets into the development or purchasing phase. The technology exists to achieve almost any goal you can define — assuming that you can afford it. If the business community does not define the goal in advance, the Solution Providers may assume that they have no performance expectations.

Exercise: Measurable Qualities

All exercises in this book are optional. They are online exercises that take anywhere from a few minutes to 20 minutes.

The next exercise will test how well you understand common subjective performance dimensions and how you can quantify them. You will see a set of performance-related statements. At the bottom of the page, you see the individual performance categories. Simply click on each statement, drag and drop it into the appropriate category to get our feedback.

To start the exercise, please go to http://goo.gl/m5MB6m

*(**DISCLAIMER:** If you attempt the exercises on a standard PC, please use IE10 or higher or Chrome. They may not work on FireFox.)*

Common Performance Measures

Now that you know how to recognize subjective performance measures and how to convert them into measurable performance statements, the next step is looking for *all* quantified requirements. You are looking for numbers.

The problem is that many Performance Requirements are not specified clearly up front. This is common since we generally think first about what we need to do and, only when we are prompted, do we start to consider how long it could or should take us to do it. Therefore, to get to a good set of Performance Requirements, you need to go back to your list of functions.

For each function on your list, you need to ask the question,

How often will this function be needed?

Express the answer as a quantity of something and a unit of time, (i.e., 150-400 times per day, 2000 – 4000 visitors per hour, weekly account updates, etc.). It is important to recognize that if different stakeholders need a function, each stakeholder may have a different answer to this question. You should ask ALL stakeholders who might use the function.

We call this the "**Frequency**" dimension and it is one of those often forgotten dimensions. In our example, we anticipate that the application will have to calculate premiums 150 and 400 times per day.

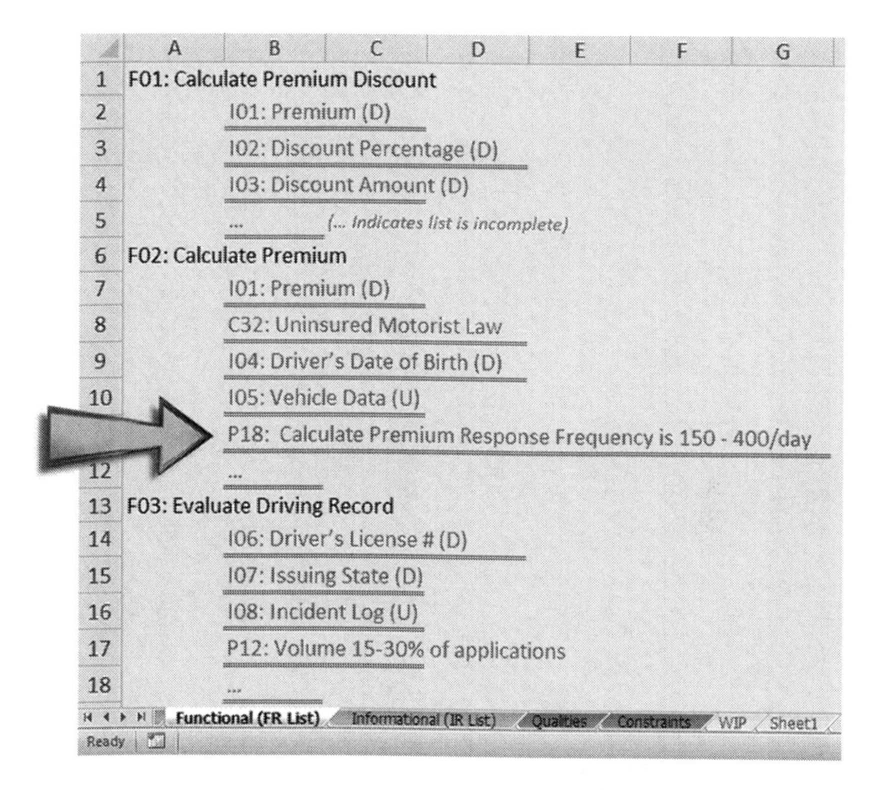

A related business dimension of functions is the "**Urgency**" dimension. For every function on your alphabetical list, you need to ask,

"When this function is performed, how quickly do the users need to know the outcome (or output), meaning how long can they wait before it impacts their job performance?"

The answer to that question is the function's "response urgency".

Interactive (on-line) applications should always have a relevant response urgency defined. Quite often the SME says something like, "We need sub-second response time." Note that "sub-second" is an upper limit (actually meaning that any time less than 1 second is good), not a specific number, but since it is dealing in such a small unit of time, it is usually sufficient.

This may not be true in real-time systems where a specific number of milliseconds or even nanoseconds might be required. In our example, the response urgency for calculating a premium is 2 seconds.

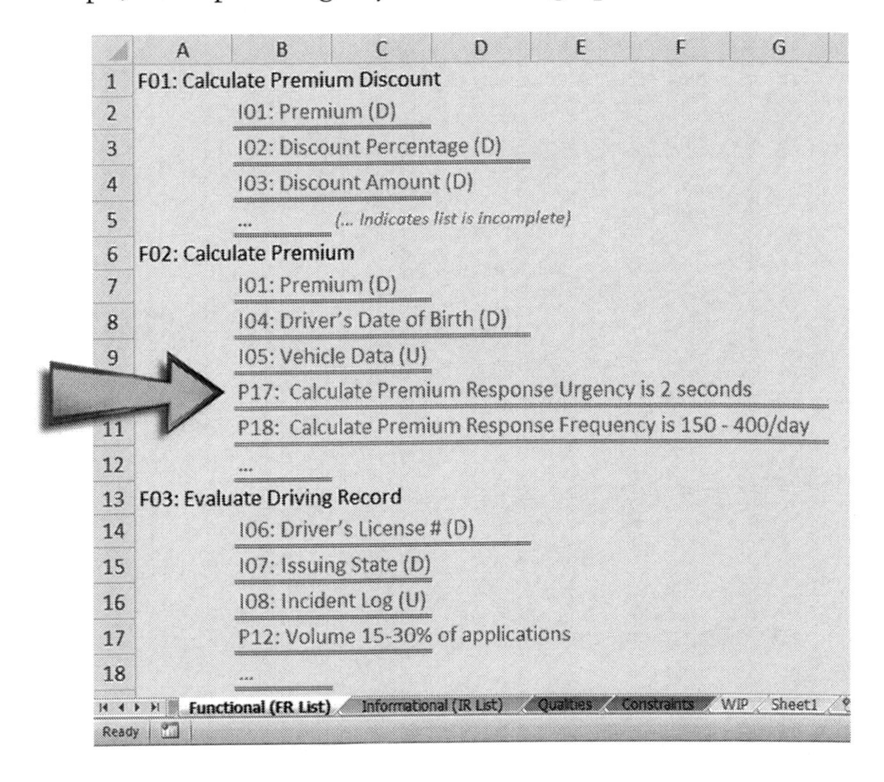

Identifying Performance-Related Functions

We discussed functional elements earlier and showed how to identify obvious and inferred functions from a Business or Stakeholder Requirement. We added the Informational Components (Data Elements and User Views with their associated attributes) created and consumed by each function.

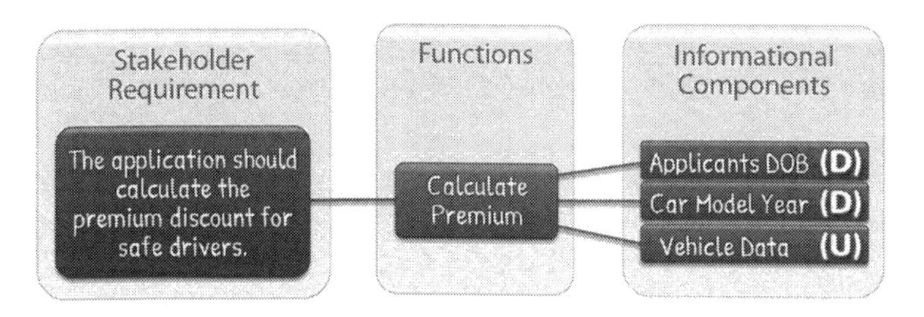

We have now discussed the importance of defining the performance expectations. Performance Requirements unveil additional functions and data that are only needed to capture, measure, and report the results.

Let us look at the Performance Requirement,

"The application has to be able to process up to 400 applications per day".

To satisfy this requirement, your solution has to include a function that counts the number of submitted applications, a function that keeps track of the time, and a function that calculate the daily totals.

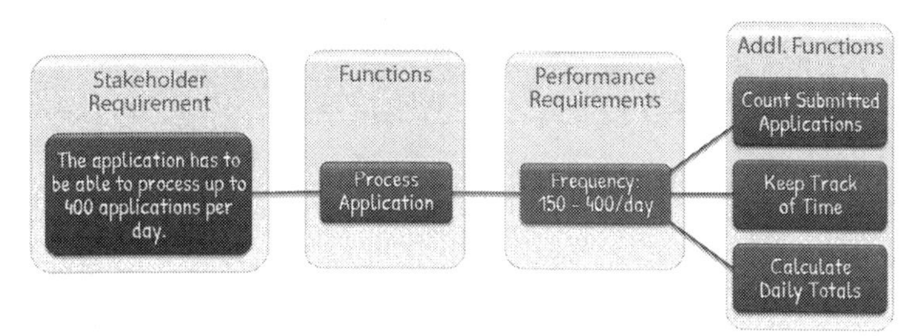

Add these performance-related functions and Informational Components to the respective lists (FR List and IR List) and capture any additional Non-Functional Requirements such as urgency, volume, accuracy, etc.

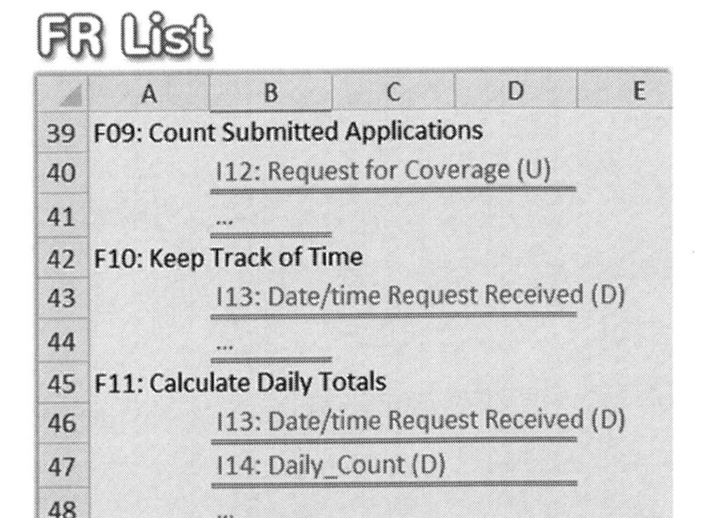

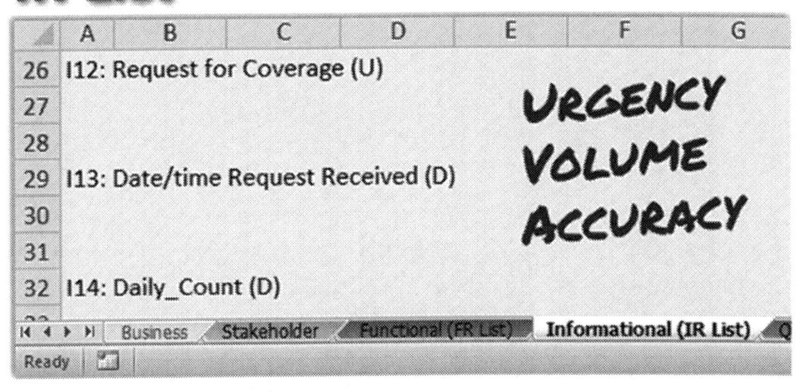

It is interesting to note that whereas the business solution might not need these functions to satisfy the stated requirements, these functions are crucial in proving whether the solution meets the defined Performance Requirements. It is also important to emphasize here that you do not need to automate all functions. If it is too complicated to automate the performance measures, a person should perform the function in the future. Adding too many automated performance measures can slow the solution down so much, that it cannot meet the critical response urgency needed.

Exercise: Discovering Performance-based Functions

All exercises in this book are optional. They are online exercises that take anywhere from a few minutes to 20 minutes.

You have here an opportunity to test your ability to identify functions needed to support Performance Requirements. We will present you with a set of Performance Requirements one at a time. For each requirement, identify as many functions that the solution would have to support to be able to measure, track, and report on the performance dimension. Type your answers followed by a comma and a space in the area provided and click on the "Submit" button to compare your answers with ours.

To start the exercise, please go to http://goo.gl/x0NpkK

(***DISCLAIMER:*** *If you attempt the exercises on a standard PC, please use IE10 or higher or Chrome. They may not work on FireFox.*)

Business Rules and External Factors

Constraints are a special category of Non-Functional Requirements that define a limit imposed by the environment in which the application will exist. To satisfy any Business, Stakeholder, Functional, or Non-Functional Requirements, Solution Providers need to know all of the internal and external constraints that affect it. External Constraints are imposed by authorities outside the control of your organization. Internal Constraints are imposed by your organization, but outside the control of your project.

For example, if you are in the health care industry dealing with personal data, the acronym "HIPAA" probably means something to you. The "Health Insurance Portability and Accountability Act" regulates (amongst other things) how parties in the health care industry exchange electronic personal data. This law is an **External Constraint** to any project that deals with personal data in the Health Care Sector. No project can change the law or can avoid it. As the one wearing the BA hat, your job is to define how the law impacts Functional and/or Informational Components of your application.

In addition, your organization can define "Business Rules" or

"Business Policies" (**Internal Constraints**) that are not subject to change by your project. These also affect your Functional and Informational Requirements. For example, an insurance company currently offers a 5% discount to drivers who have not had a traffic violation or accident within the past three years. The **5%** and **three** years are both values that are **subject to change at any time**. You need to communicate to the Solution Providers that the business community needs to maintain these values without the need to modify the application's code.

For any given Functional or Informational Component, you need to identify all applicable laws and regulations that define what a function must do, what it must not do, or that place restrictions on the Informational Component. Those are External Constraints.

In addition, you need to take a look at business rules, policies, and procedures that might affect the function or data. Make sure that you document these constraints and reference them in all impacted Functional and Informational Requirements.

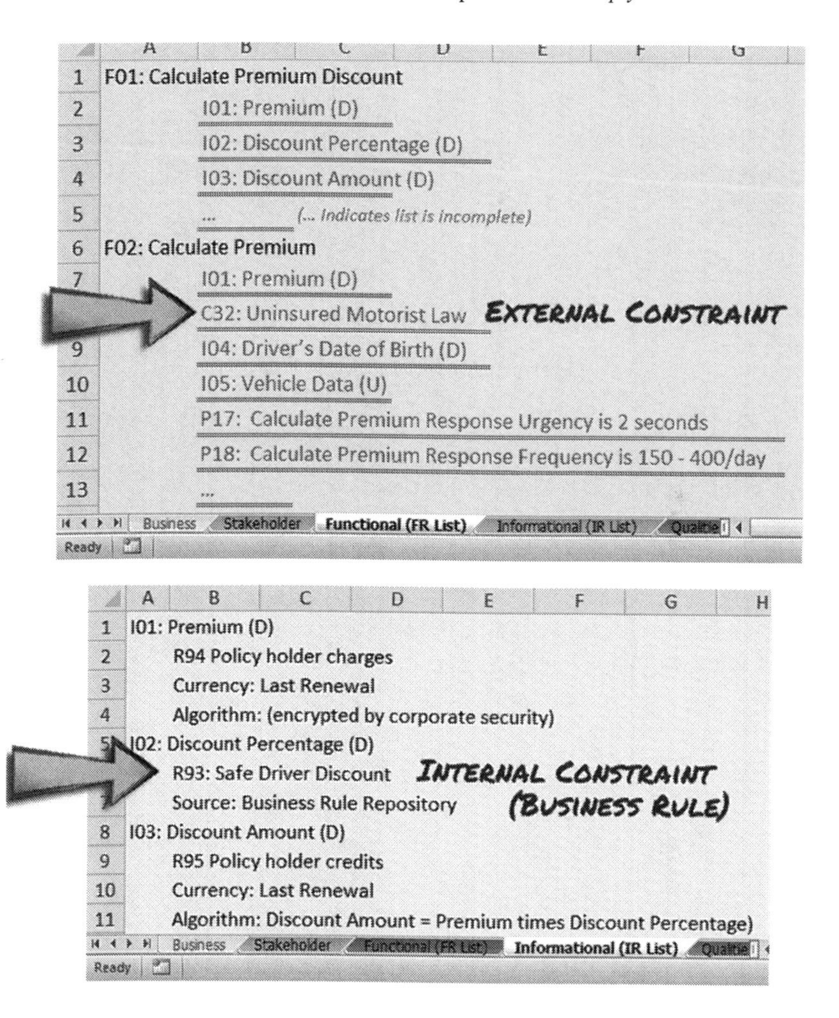
F01: Calculate Premium Discount
I01: Premium (D)
I02: Discount Percentage (D)
I03: Discount Amount (D)
... (... Indicates list is incomplete)
F02: Calculate Premium
I01: Premium (D)
C32: Uninsured Motorist Law
EXTERNAL CONSTRAINT
I04: Driver's Date of Birth (D)
I05: Vehicle Data (U)
P17: Calculate Premium Response Urgency is 2 seconds
P18: Calculate Premium Response Frequency is 150 - 400/day
...
Business
Stakeholder
Functional (FR List)
Informational (IR List)
Ready
I01: Premium (D)
R94 Policy holder charges
Currency: Last Renewal
Algorithm: (encrypted by corporate security)
I02: Discount Percentage (D)
R93: Safe Driver Discount
INTERNAL CONSTRAINT
Source: Business Rule Repository
(BUSINESS RULE)
I03: Discount Amount (D)
R95 Policy holder credits
Currency: Last Renewal
Algorithm: Discount Amount = Premium times Discount Percentage)
Business
Stakeholder
Functional (FR List)
Informational (IR List)
Ready

Discovering Constraining Requirements

Look at a concrete example of constraints. We referenced the requirement,

---

"The application should calculate the premium discount of 5% for drivers who have not had an accident in the past three years."

Using techniques discussed previously, you identified several functional elements, namely "Calculate Discount", "Determine Accident-Free Years", etc. and several Data Elements like "Premium", "Discount Amount", "Accident History", and so on. Your next step is to identify any stakeholder that has authority to mandate how these functions work or what data the function creates.

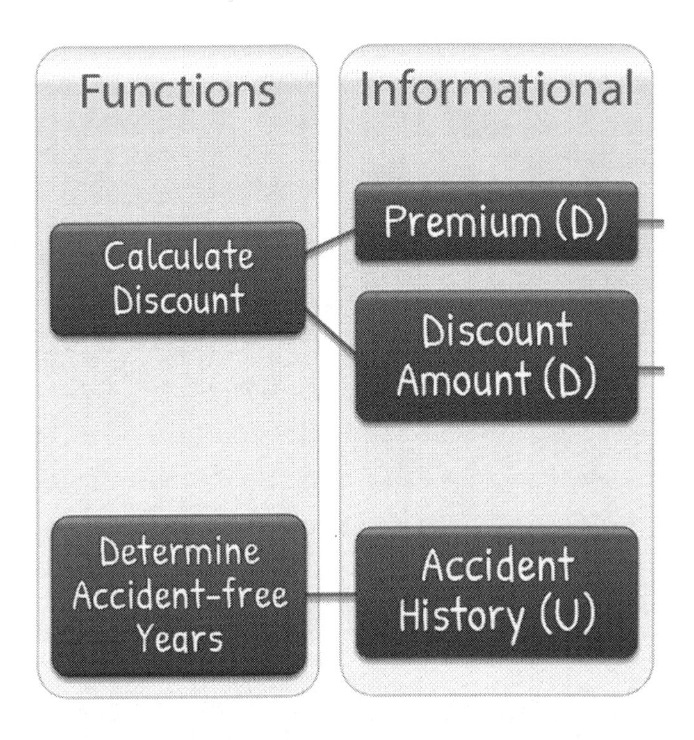

As you dig deeper, you discover that the company cannot change

the Data Element "Premium" without the approval by a state insurance board. That means there is an External Constraint under the control of a regulatory agency that the "Premium" has to come from an "Approved Rate Table".

Next, we are informed that the "Discount Amount" is currently 5% but subject to change by the business community. This is an Internal Constraint (aka Business Rule) affecting the Data Element and the functions that create it.

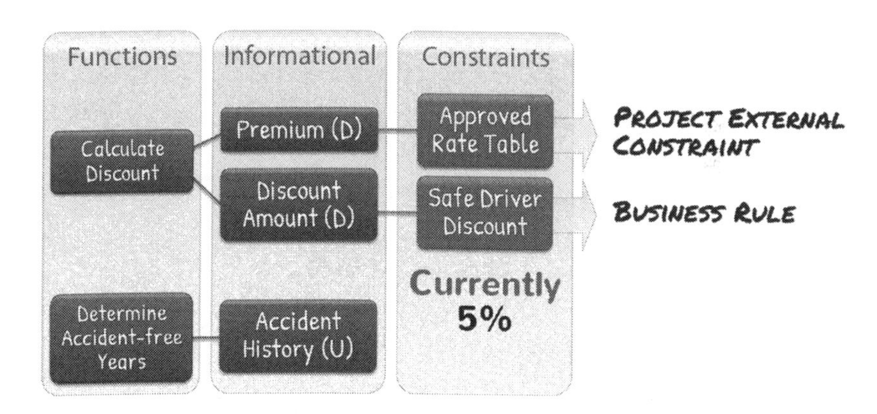

You previously connected each Data Element to the functions that create or consume it. By associating the constraint or rule with the data component, you are automatically "constraining" the related functions. Since each constraint may impact multiple functions, we recommend documenting the External and Internal Constraints in one place and referencing them in each impacted Functional or Informational Requirement.

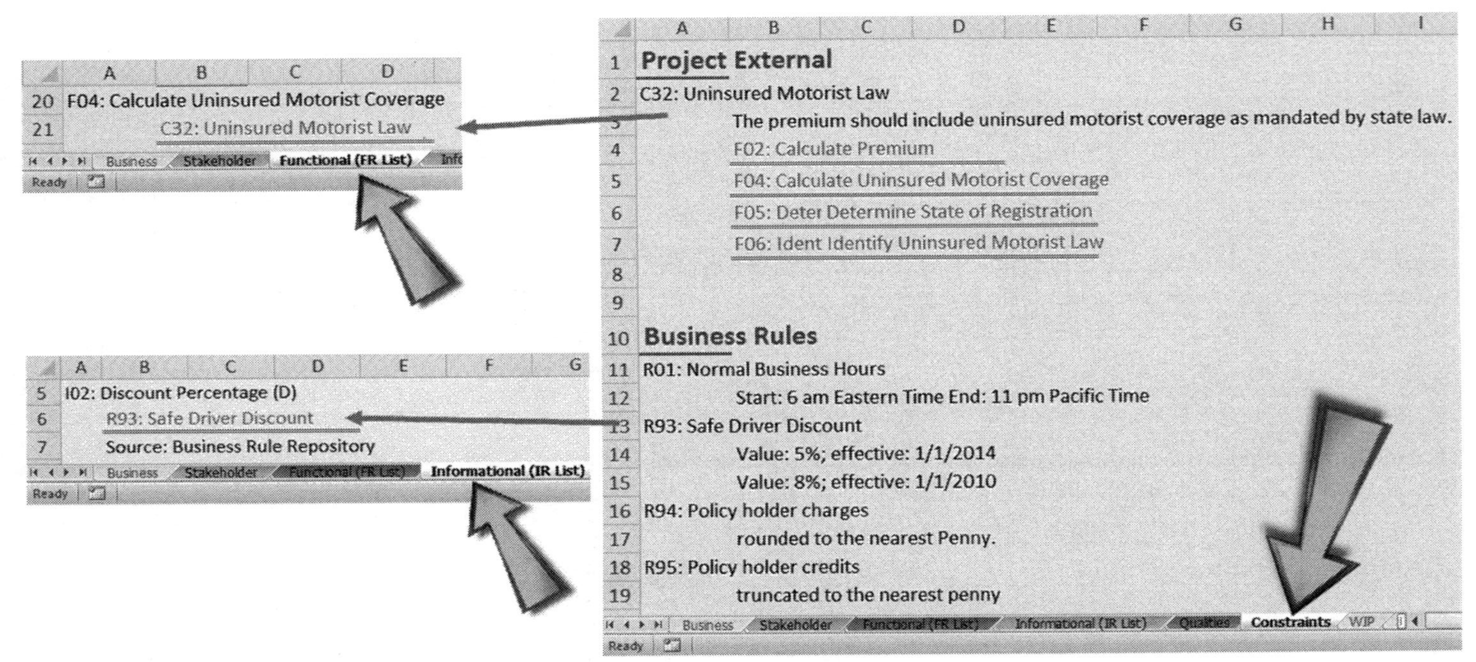
F04: Calculate Uninsured Motorist Coverage
C32: Uninsured Motorist Law
Business
Stakeholder
Functional (FR List)
Ready
I02: Discount Percentage (D)
R93: Safe Driver Discount
Source: Business Rule Repository
Business
Stakeholder
Functional (FR List)
Informational (IR List)
Ready
Project External
C32: Uninsured Motorist Law
The premium should include uninsured motorist coverage as mandated by state law.
F02: Calculate Premium
F04: Calculate Uninsured Motorist Coverage
F05: Deter Determine State of Registration
F06: Ident Identify Uninsured Motorist Law
Business Rules
R01: Normal Business Hours
Start: 6 am Eastern Time End: 11 pm Pacific Time
R93: Safe Driver Discount
Value: 5%; effective: 1/1/2014
Value: 8%; effective: 1/1/2010
R94: Policy holder charges
rounded to the nearest Penny.
R95: Policy holder credits
truncated to the nearest penny
Business
Stakeholder
Functional (FR List)
Informational (IR List)
Qualities
Constraints
WIP
Ready

Online resources for you:

- ⇨ Non-Functional Requirements Add Value to User Stories
https://www.youtube.com/watch?v=NnD7UhnIsNc

- ⇨ Non-functional Requirements as User Stories
https://www.mountaingoatsoftware.com/blog/non-functional-requirements-as-user-stories

- ⇨ Scaled Agile Framework: Nonfunctional Requirements
http://scaledagileframework.com/nonfunctional-requirements/

- ⇨ How to write Performance Requirements with Example
http://www.1202performance.com/atricles/how-to-write-performance-requirements-with-example/

- ⇨ Performance Requirements: An Attempt of a Systematic View
http://www.alexanderpodelko.com/docs/PerfRequirements_CMG11.pdf

- ⇨ Business Rules vs. Business Requirements: Are you confused?
http://www.brcommunity.com/b290.php

- ⇨ Business Rules: An Agile Introduction
http://agilemodeling.com/artifacts/businessRule.htm

- ⇨ Constraints: An Agile Introduction
http://www.agilemodeling.com/artifacts/constraint.htm

- ⇨ Your Personalized Business Analysis Skills Evaluation
http://businessanalysisexperts.com/BASE/business-analyst-skills-self-assessment.html

- ⇨ FREE Business Analysis Videos
http://businessanalysisexperts.com/product-category/free-business-analysis-training/

IN CLOSING

Requirements Management Ideas

We introduced several different types of "Solution Requirements" (Functional, Informational, Performance, Constraints). We also recommended creating separate and searchable lists (FR List, IR List, etc.) for each type of requirement to avoid redundancy that causes discrepancies and disconnects (two of the major problems in requirements documentation).

Having all of those lists can be confusing, so we introduced a simple spreadsheet solution using Microsoft Excel as a requirements repository. If you use our tool, you will see tabs labeled "Business", "Stakeholder", "Functional", "Informational", "Qualities", "Constraints", and "WIP".

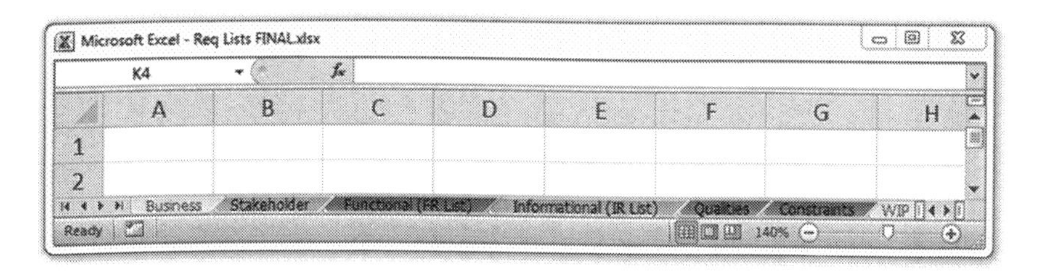

The first four tabs and "Constraints" are self-explanatory based on the presented concepts. The "Qualities" tab contains Performance Requirements that you can relate to multiple functions. We named it "Qualities" to encompass additional, measurable types of requirements (e.g., "Availability", "Reliability", and "Learnability").

If you document these Qualities on their own tab, you ensure that any future change shows up wherever these requirement types are referenced. The final tab "WIP" is simply a place to put requirements that need further analysis. Once you have decomposed the requirement, we recommend removing it from the WIP tab. Although our tool is sufficient for smaller projects, it will quickly deteriorate to a mess as the number of requirements increases.

The good news is that there are a number of "Requirements Management" tools available on the market and pretty much any of them will maintain relationships between the various types of requirements. In the interest of providing you with unbiased information, we do not endorse or recommend any commercially available Requirements Management tool. However, we have listed a few sources in the "*Online resources for you*" section at the end of this chapter.

We do suggest that if you decide to acquire such a tool, you need to define your requirements for the tool before you buy one. From the BA perspective, implementing a Requirements Management tool in your organization is just another project that needs all of the upfront work to avoid downstream problems. Search the web for current Requirements Management tools.

If you do not want or cannot afford a commercial requirements management tool, our little spreadsheet might satisfy your needs. Simply create a workbook and add a tab for each requirement type. To ensure consistency when requirements change (and they will), we strongly recommend that you maintain the linkage between requirement types as opposed to cutting and pasting the values.

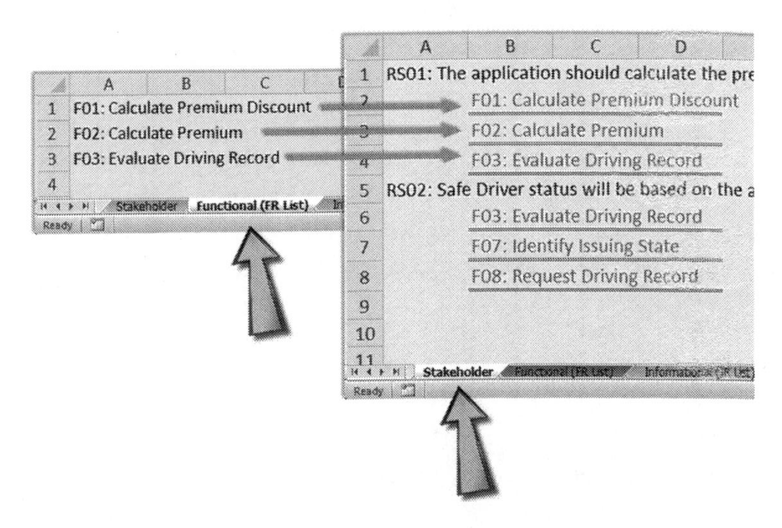

Process and Rule Review

To deliver a solution that meets the defined Business and Stakeholder Requirements, Solution Providers need both the Functional and Non-Functional Requirements at the appropriate (measurable) level of detail. In this section, we have introduced some examples of non-functional categories that may or may not work for your situation. Because the non-functional dimension depends entirely on your environment, the one wearing the BA hat has to figure out which Non-Functional Requirements are critical for their project.

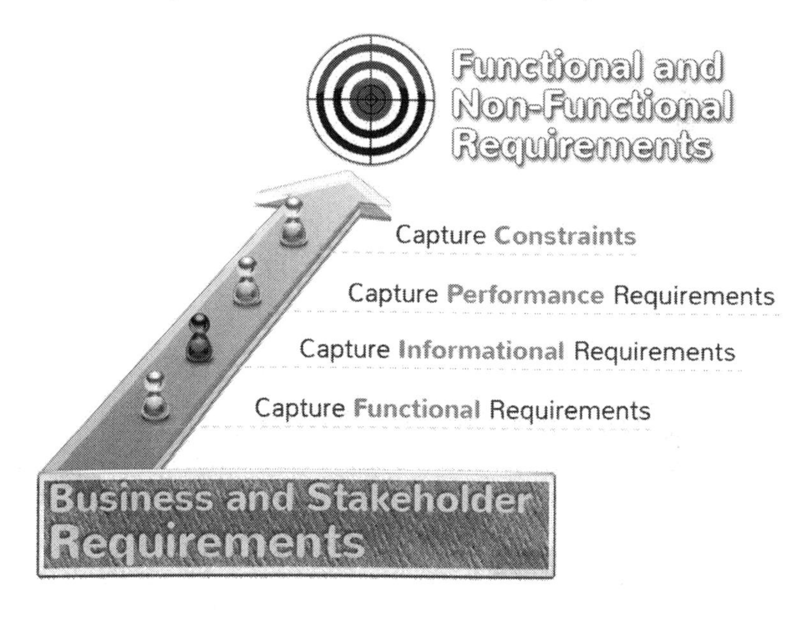

You now own a repeatable process for deriving Functional and Non-Functional Requirements (aka Solution Requirements) from Business and Stakeholder Requirements that meet our four rules for writing effective requirement statements. The described approach serves to minimize misinterpretation of the Business and Stakeholder Requirement statements by Solution Providers.

To summarize: An effective requirement decomposes to Functional and Non-Functional components defined in measurable terms specifying:

- ☑ Functions the solution will perform (manual and automated actions)
- ☑ Data the functions manipulate or present (e.g., Data Elements, User Views)
- ☑ Attributes of all new Informational Components (e.g., owner, precision, source, algorithm)
- ☑ Behavioral qualities (e.g., performance, availability, usability, reliability, maintainability, adaptability)
- ☑ Constraints imposed on the overall solution or any of its components (e.g., laws, regulations, standards, business rules, policies, security)

If you follow these simple steps, your Business Requirements will provide the Solution Providers the guidance they need to make appropriate trade-off decisions. Making sure that your Solution Requirements are measurable will lead in the end to the delivery of verifiably acceptable business solutions to the business community.

Reading and listening is great for building awareness, but people do not really learn any new skill until they do it. You will get a lot more out of this course if you now flex your knowledge muscle by checking your understanding of this process in our “final exam”.

Exercise: Final Exam

All exercises in this book are optional. They are online exercises that take anywhere from a few minutes to 20 minutes.

This exercise will test your understanding of the various requirement components covered in this book. You will have a set of individual requirement statements. For each statement, we will give you two categories of components that you need to find. Simply type your answers (separated, as always, with a comma and a space) into the respective text area and click on the "Submit" button when you are done.

To start the exercise, please go to http://goo.gl/cXKjL5

*(**DISCLAIMER:** If you attempt the exercises on a standard PC, please use IE10 or higher or Chrome. They may not work on FireFox.)*

What Should You Do Next?

Thank you for reading, "Functional and Non-Functional Requirements – *Simply Put!*". We trust that you enjoyed the book, hope that you are able to integrate the presented ideas into your life, and that they serve you well when you are the one wearing the business analysis hat.

Any feedback you provide helps us improve the learning experience for all students. Please write a review on Amazon or our website to capture your feedback. If you have any issues to report, we will respond as quickly as possible.

This book is just one component of our blended learning curriculum. Our discovery learning-based training approach and our other delivery methods (onsite/online classroom, self-paced eCourses, eBooks, and eMentoring) augment books such as this and allow you to select the appropriate combination to build your business analysis skills while containing costs. Check our Business Analysis Training Store (http://businessanalysisexperts.com/business-analysis-training-store/) for a complete overview of all of our training offers for the one wearing the BA hat.

Meanwhile, thank you again for buying this book. Use your new-found business analysis knowledge to achieve your personal and professional goals.

Online resources for you:

- ⇨ Webinar: Requirements Management Best Practices
  https://www.youtube.com/watch?v=7vx6RDydAPo

- ⇨ Do you know? "7 Practices" for a Reliable Requirements Management
  http://www.raquest.com/downloads/SevenPracticesForRM.pdf

- ⇨ Managing Requirements through the Lifecycle of an Agile Project
  https://www.youtube.com/watch?v=OnZleFmrXoU

- ⇨ List of Requirements Management Tools
  http://makingofsoftware.com/resources/list-of-rm-tools

- ⇨ The IIBA introduces 2 Requirements Management tools that manage non-functional requirements (be patient when downloading. This is a fairly large pdf file)
  http://www.iiba.org/Learning-Development/Vendor-Showcase/2013/2013-12-12-non-functional-requirements-analysis.aspx

- ⇨ Agile Requirements Change Management
  http://agilemodeling.com/essays/changeManagement.htm

- ⇨ Why Agile Requirements Tools are the Future, According to Forrester
  http://www.blueprintsys.com/why-agile-requirements-tools-are-the-future/

ABOUT THE AUTHORS

Angela and Tom Hathaway have authored and delivered hundreds of training courses and publications for business analysts around the world. They have facilitated hundreds of requirements discovery sessions for information technology projects under a variety of acronyms (JAD, ASAP, JADr, JRP, etc.). Based on their personal journey and experiences reported by their students, they recognized how much anyone can benefit from improving their requirements elicitation skills.

Angela's and Tom's mission is to allow anyone, anywhere access to simple, easy-to-learn business analysis techniques by sharing their experience and expertise in their business analysis training seminars, blogs, books, and public presentations.

At BA-EXPERTS (http://businessanalysisexperts.com/) we focus exclusively on Business Analysis for **"anyone wearing the BA hat™"**. We believe that business analysis has become a needed skill for every business professional whether or not they have the title Business Analyst. We have made it our goal to enable anyone wearing the BA hat™ to have access to high quality training material and performance support. Please call us at 702-637-4573, email us (Tom.Hathaway@ba-experts.com), or visit our Business Analyst Learning Store at (http://businessanalysisexperts.com/business-analysis-training-store/) if you are interested in other training offers. Amongst other offers, the content of this book is also available as an eCourse on our website.

19785821R00040

Made in the USA
Middletown, DE
07 December 2018